A GIFT *for*

....

FROM

....

GOD'S MESSAGE OF

Christmas

Love

EUGENE H. PETERSON

Copyright © 2004 by Eugene H. Peterson.

Published by J. Countryman, a division of Thomas Nelson, Inc, Nashville, Tennessee 37214.

Published in association with the literary agency of Alive Communications, Inc.,
1465 Kelly Johnson Blvd., Suite 320, Colorado Springs, CO 80920.

Project manager—Terri Gibbs

Scripture quotations in this book are from THE MESSAGE, © 1993, 1994, 1995, 1996, 2000, 2001, 2002. Used by permission of the NavPress Publishing Group.

Designed by The DesignWorks Group, Sisters, Oregon. www.thedesignworksgroup.com

ISBN: 1-4041-0132-2

www.thomasnelson.com
www.jcountryman.com
www.messagebible.com

Printed and bound in the United States of America

GOD is great,
and worth a thousand Hallelujahs.

PSALM 96:4

What do Bible stories tell us about living this human life well, living it totally? Primarily and mostly they tell us that it means dealing with God. Always, at the forefront and in the background of circumstances, events, and people, it's God.

In the pages of scripture we see the acts of salvation, of providence, of blessing. . . . We see God entering our history in the form of a servant.

Though there were auspicious signs that preceded and accompanied his birth, preparing the world for the majestic and kingly, the birth of Jesus itself was of the humblest peasant parentage, in an unimportant town, and in the roughest of buildings. He made a career of rejecting marks of status or privilege. Everything about Jesus spoke of servitude.

Good tidings. Good news. Gospel.

This gospel is not just any good news— . . . it is the unexpected, fresh, surprising good news that God loves and has provided the means for our salvation. God's love and our salvation are completely expressed and fully accomplished in Jesus Christ. That is good news.

God is generous and never runs out of blessings. God delights in giving—it's what he does best. But his love is passionate and seeks faithful, committed love in return.

At the Christmas season and throughout the year, may we respond to God's love and God's Word with a heart like Mary, who humbly and willingly said: "Let it be with me just as you say" (Luke 1:38).

—EUGENE H. PETERSON

GOD'S MESSAGE OF

Christmas

Love

Come to Bethlehem and see

Him whose birth the angels sing;

come, adore on bended knee

Christ the Lord, the new-born King.

God's love
and our salvation are
completely expressed and fully
accomplished in Jesus Christ.
That is good news.

—EUGENE H. PETERSON

Silent Night, Holy Night

JOSEPH MOHR 1792–1848

Silent night! holy night!
all is calm, all is bright
round yon virgin mother and Child,
holy Infant, so tender and mild—
sleep in heavenly peace, sleep in heavenly peace.

Silent night! holy night!
shepherds quake at the sight;
glories stream from heaven afar;
heav'nly hosts sing alleluia—
Christ the Savior is born! Christ the Savior is born!

Silent night! holy night!
Son of God, love's pure light,
radiant beams from Thy holy face,
with the dawn of redeeming grace—
Jesus, Lord at Thy birth, Jesus, Lord at Thy birth.

A VIRGIN CONCEIVES

od sent the angel Gabriel to the Galilean village of Nazareth to a virgin engaged to be married to a man descended from David. His name was Joseph, and the virgin's name, Mary. Upon entering, Gabriel greeted her:

Good morning!
You're beautiful with God's beauty,
Beautiful inside and out!
God be with you.

She was thoroughly shaken, wondering what was behind a greeting like that. But the angel assured her, "Mary, you have nothing to fear. God has a surprise for you:

You will become pregnant and give birth to a son and call his name Jesus.

> *He will be great,*
> *be called 'Son of the Highest.'*
> *The Lord God will give him*
> *the throne of his father David;*
> *He will rule Jacob's house forever—*
> *no end, ever, to his kingdom."*

Mary said to the angel, "But how? I've never slept with a man."
The angel answered,

> *The Holy Spirit will come upon you,*
> *the power of the Highest hover over you;*
> *Therefore, the child you bring to birth*
> *will be called Holy, Son of God.*

"And did you know that your cousin Elizabeth conceived a son, old as she is? Everyone called her barren, and here she is six months' pregnant! Nothing, you see, is impossible with God."

The Master

is going to give you a sign anyway.
Watch for this:
A girl who is presently a virgin
will get pregnant.
She'll bear a son and name him
Immanuel (God-With-Us).

ISAIAH 7:14

And Mary said,

> Yes, I see it all now:
> I'm the Lord's maid, ready to serve.
> Let it be with me
> just as you say.

Then the angel left her.

(Luke 1:1–38)

God not only
speaks to us, he listens to us.
His listening to us
is an even greater marvel than
his speaking to us.

—EUGENE H. PETERSON

Angels We Have Heard On High

18TH CENTURY FRENCH CAROL

Angels we have heard on high,
sweetly singing o'er the plains,
and the mountains, in reply,
echoing their joyous strains.

Shepherds, why this jubilee?
Why your joyous strains prolong?
What the gladsome tidings be
which inspire your heav'nly song?

Come to Bethlehem and see
Him whose birth the angels sing;
come, adore on bended knee
Christ the Lord, the new-born King.

See Him in a manger laid,
Jesus, Lord of heav'n and earth;
Mary, Joseph, lend your aid,
with us sing our Savior's birth.

REFRAIN: Gloria in excelsis Deo!

BLESSED AMONG WOMEN

Mary didn't waste a minute. She got up and traveled to a town in Judah in the hill country, straight to Zachariah's house, and greeted Elizabeth. When Elizabeth heard Mary's greeting, the baby in her womb leaped. She was filled with the Holy Spirit, and sang out exuberantly,

You're so blessed among women,
and the babe in your womb, also blessed!
And why am I so blessed that
the mother of my Lord visits me?
The moment the sound of your
greeting entered my ears,
The babe in my womb
skipped like a lamb for sheer joy.
Blessed woman, who believed what God said,
believed every word would come true!

God sent me

to announce the year of his grace. . .

give them bouquets of roses

instead of ashes,

messages of joy instead of

news of doom.

ISAIAH 61:2, 3

And Mary said,

I'm bursting with God-news;
I'm dancing the song of my Savior God.
God took one good look at me, and look what happened—
I'm the most fortunate woman on earth!
What God has done for me will never be forgotten,
the God whose very name is holy, set apart from all others.
His mercy flows in wave after wave
on those who are in awe before him.
He bared his arm and showed his strength,
scattered the bluffing braggarts.
He knocked tyrants off their high horses,
pulled victims out of the mud.
The starving poor sat down to a banquet;
the callous rich were left out in the cold.
He embraced his chosen child, Israel;
he remembered and piled on the mercies, piled them high.
It's exactly what he promised,
beginning with Abraham and right up to now.

Mary stayed with Elizabeth for three months and then went back to her own home.

(Luke 1:39–56)

This is GOD's work.
We rub our eyes—we can
hardly believe it!

PSALM 118:23

To believe
in a miracle is only a way of
saying that God is free—
free to do a new thing.

—EUGENE H. PETERSON

Away in a Manger

JOHN THOMAS McFARLAND 1851–1913

Away in a manger,
no crib for a bed,
the little Lord Jesus laid down His sweet head;
the stars in the sky looked down where He lay,
the little Lord Jesus, asleep on the hay.

The cattle are lowing;
the Baby awakes,
but little Lord Jesus, no crying He makes;
I love Thee, Lord Jesus! Look down from the sky,
and stay by my cradle till morning is nigh.

Be near me, Lord Jesus,
I ask Thee to stay
close by me forever, and love me, I pray;
bless all the dear children in Thy tender care,
and fit us for heaven, to live with Thee there.

THE BIRTH OF JESUS

T he birth of Jesus took place like this. His mother, Mary, was engaged to be married to Joseph. Before they came to the marriage bed, Joseph discovered she was pregnant. (It was by the Holy Spirit, but he didn't know that.) Joseph, chagrined but noble, determined to take care of things quietly so Mary would not be disgraced.

While he was trying to figure a way out, he had a dream. God's angel spoke in the dream: "Joseph, son of David, don't hesitate to get married. Mary's pregnancy is Spirit-conceived. God's Holy Spirit has made her pregnant. She will bring a son to birth, and when she does, you, Joseph, will name him Jesus—'God saves'—because he will save his people from their sins." This would bring the prophet's embryonic sermon to full term:

> *Watch for this—a virgin will get pregnant and bear a son;*
> *They will name him Emmanuel (Hebrew for "God is with us").*

Then Joseph woke up. He did exactly what God's angel commanded in the dream. *(Matthew 1:18–24)*

About that time Caesar Augustus ordered a census to be taken throughout the Empire. This was the first census when Quirinius was governor of Syria. Everyone had to travel to his own ancestral hometown to be accounted for. So Joseph went from the Galilean town of Nazareth up to Bethlehem in Judah, David's town, for the census. As a descendant of David, he had to go there. He went with Mary, his fiancée, who was pregnant.

> BUT YOU BETHLEHEM,
> DAVID'S COUNTRY,
> THE RUNT OF THE
> LITTER—
> FROM YOU WILL
> COME THE LEADER
> WHO WILL
> SHEPHERD-RULE ISRAEL.
> MICAH 5:2

While they were there, the time came for her to give birth. She gave birth to a son, her firstborn. She wrapped him in a blanket and laid him in a manger, because there was no room in the hostel.

(Luke 2:1–7)

God gets down
on his knees among us,
gets on our level
and shares himself with us.

EUGENE H. PETERSON

O Little Town of Bethlehem

PHILLIPS BROOKS 1835–1893

O little town of Bethlehem,
how still we see thee lie!
Above thy deep and dreamless sleep
the silent stars go by;
yet in thy dark streets shineth
the everlasting Light—
the hopes and fears of all the years
are met in thee tonight.

For Christ is born of Mary—
and gathered all above,
while mortals sleep,
the angels keep their watch of wond'ring love.
O morning stars,
together proclaim the holy birth,
and praises sing to God the King,
and peace to men on earth.

How silently, how silently
the wondrous gift is giv'n!
So God imparts to human hearts
the blessings of His heav'n.
No ear may hear His coming,
but, in this world of sin,
where meek souls will receive Him still
the dear Christ enters in.

O holy Child of Bethlehem
descend to us, we pray;
cast out our sin and enter in—
be born in us today.
We hear the Christmas angels
the great glad tidings tell;
O come to us, abide with us,
our Lord Emmanuel!

An Event for Everyone

Like a shepherd, he will care for his flock,
gathering the lambs in his arms,
hugging them as he carries them,
leading the nursing ewes to good pasture.

ISAIAH 40:11

There were sheepherders camping in the neighborhood. They had set night watches over their sheep. Suddenly, God's angel stood among them and God's glory blazed around them. They were terrified. The angel said, "Don't be afraid. I'm here to announce a great and joyful event that is meant for everybody, worldwide: A Savior has just been born in David's town, a Savior who is Messiah and Master. This is what you're to look for: a baby wrapped in a blanket and lying in a manger."

At once the angel was joined by a huge angelic choir singing God's praises:

Glory to God in the heavenly heights,
Peace to all men and women on earth who please him.

As the angel choir withdrew into heaven, the sheepherders talked it over. "Let's get over to Bethlehem as fast as we can and see for ourselves what God has revealed to us." They left, running, and found Mary and Joseph, and the baby lying in the manger. Seeing was believing. They told everyone they met what the angels had said about this child. All who heard the sheepherders were impressed.

Mary kept all these things to herself, holding them dear, deep within herself. The sheepherders returned and let loose, glorifying and praising God for everything they had heard and seen. It turned out exactly the way they'd been told!

(Luke 2:8–20)

YOUR LOVE,

GOD, IS MY SONG,

AND I'LL SING IT!

I'M FOREVER TELLING

EVERYONE HOW FAITHFUL

YOU ARE.

PSALM 89:1

The whole earth comes to attention.
Look—God's work of salvation!

Shout your praises to God, everybody!
Let loose and sing! Strike up the band!

Round up an orchestra to play for GOD,
Add a hundred-voice choir.

Feature trumpets and big trombones,
Fill the air with praises to King GOD.

PSALM 98:4–7

A child has been born—for us!

The gift of a son—for us!

He'll take over the running of the world.

His names will be:

Amazing Counselor,

Strong God, Eternal Father,

Prince of Wholeness.

His ruling authority will grow,

and there'll be no limits to the

wholeness he brings.

ISAIAH 9:6–7

Joy to the World

ISAAC WATTS 1674–1748

Joy to the world! The Lord is come!
Let earth receive her King;
let ev'ry heart prepare Him room,
and heav'n and nature sing.

Joy to the earth! The Savior reigns.
Let men their songs employ,
while fields and floods, rocks, hills and plains
repeat the sounding joy.

No more let sins and sorrows grow,
nor thorns infest the ground;
He comes to make His blessings flow
far as the curse is found.

He rules the world with truth and grace,
and makes the nations prove
the glories of His righteousness
and wonders of His love.

BLESSINGS

hen the eighth day arrived, the day of circumcision, the child was named Jesus, the name given by the angel before he was conceived.

Then when the days stipulated by Moses for purification were complete, they took him up to Jerusalem to offer him to God as commanded in God's Law: "Every male who opens the womb shall be a holy offering to God," and also to sacrifice the "pair of doves or two young pigeons" prescribed in God's Law.

In Jerusalem at the time, there was a man, Simeon by name, a good man, a man who lived in the prayerful expectancy of help for Israel. And the Holy Spirit was on him. The Holy Spirit had shown him that he would see the Messiah of

God before he died. Led by the Spirit, he entered the Temple. As the parents of the child Jesus brought him in to carry out the rituals of the Law, Simeon took him into his arms and blessed God:

> *God, you can now release your servant;*
> *release me in peace as you promised.*
> *With my own eyes I've seen your salvation;*
> *it's now out in the open for everyone to see:*
> *A God-revealing light to the non-Jewish nations,*
> *and of glory for your people Israel.*

Jesus' father and mother were speechless with surprise at these words. Simeon went on to bless them, and said to Mary his mother,

> *This child marks both the failure and*
> *the recovery of many in Israel,*
> *A figure misunderstood and contradicted—*
> *the pain of a sword-thrust through you—*
> *But the rejection will force honesty,*
> *as God reveals who they really are.*

I lift you high in praise,
my God, O my King!
And I'll bless your name
into eternity.

PSALM 145:1

Anna the prophetess was also there, a daughter of Phanuel from the tribe of Asher. She was by now a very old woman. She had been married seven years and a widow for eighty-four. She never left the Temple area, worshiping night and day with her fastings and prayers. At the very time Simeon was praying, she showed up, broke into an anthem of praise to God, and talked about the child to all who were waiting expectantly for the freeing of Jerusalem.

When they finished everything required by God in the Law, they returned to Galilee and their own town, Nazareth.

(Luke 2:21–39)

As we acquire good things
in our lives we do not become more
and more independent.
We do not build larger storehouses
in order to preserve our riches;
we find new outlets for sharing,
for helping, for giving.

—EUGENE H. PETERSON

We Three Kings

JOHN H. HOPKINS, 1820–1891

We three kings of Orient are,
bearing gifts we traverse afar,
field and fountain, moor and mountain,
following yonder star.

Born a King on Bethlehem's plain,
gold I bring to crown Him again,
King forever, ceasing never
over us all to reign.

Frankincense to offer have I;
incense owns a Deity nigh;
prayer and praising, all men raising,
worship Him, God on high.

Myrrh is mine; its bitter perfume
breathes a life of gathering gloom:

Sorr'wing, sighing, bleeding, dying,
sealed in the stone-cold tomb.

Glorious now
behold Him arise,
King and God and Sacrifice; alleluia, alleluia!
peals through the earth and skies.

Scholars from the East

After Jesus was born in Bethlehem village, Judah territory—this was during Herod's kingship—a band of scholars arrived in Jerusalem from the East. They asked around, "Where can we find and pay homage to the newborn King of the Jews? We observed a star in the eastern sky that signaled his birth. We're on pilgrimage to worship him."

When word of their inquiry got to Herod, he was terrified—and not Herod alone, but most of Jerusalem as well. Herod lost no time. He gathered all the high priests and religion scholars in the city together and asked, "Where is the Messiah supposed to be born?"

They told him, "Bethlehem, Judah territory. The prophet Micah wrote it plainly:

It's you, Bethlehem, in Judah's land,
no longer bringing up the rear.
From you will come the leader
who will shepherd-rule my people, my Israel."

Herod then arranged a secret meeting with the scholars from the East. Pretending to be as devout as they were, he got them to tell him exactly when the birth-announcement star appeared. Then he told them the prophecy about Bethlehem, and said, "Go find this child. Leave no stone unturned. As soon as you find him, send word and I'll join you at once in your worship."

Instructed by the king, they set off. Then the star appeared again, the same star they had seen in the eastern skies. It led them on until it hovered over the place of the child. They could hardly contain themselves: They were in the right place! They had arrived at the right time!

They entered the house and saw the child in the arms of Mary, his mother. Overcome, they knelt and worshiped him. Then they opened their luggage and presented gifts: gold, frankincense, myrrh.

In a dream, they were warned not to report back to Herod. So they worked out another route, left the territory without being seen, and returned to their own country.

After the scholars were gone, God's angel showed up again in Joseph's dream and commanded, "Get up. Take the child and his mother and flee to Egypt. Stay until further notice. Herod is on the hunt for this child, and wants to kill him."

Bring gifts and celebrate,
Bow before the beauty of GOD,
Then to your knees—everyone worship!

PSALM 96:7

Joseph obeyed. He got up, took the child and his mother under cover of darkness. They were out of town and well on their way by daylight. They lived in Egypt until Herod's death. This Egyptian exile fulfilled what Hosea had preached: "I called my son out of Egypt."

Herod, when he realized that the scholars had tricked him, flew into a rage. He commanded the murder of every little boy two years old and under who lived in Bethlehem and its surrounding hills. (He determined that age from information he'd gotten from the scholars.) That's when Jeremiah's sermon was fulfilled:

> *A sound was heard in Ramah,*
> *weeping and much lament.*
> *Rachel weeping for her children,*
> *Rachel refusing all solace,*
> *Her children gone,*
> *dead and buried.*

Later, when Herod died, God's angel appeared in a dream to Joseph in Egypt: "Up, take the child and his mother and return to Israel. All those out to murder the child are dead."

Joseph obeyed. He got up, took the child and his mother, and reentered Israel. When he heard, though, that Archelaus had succeeded his father, Herod, as king in Judea, he was afraid to go there. But then Joseph was directed in a dream to go to the hills of Galilee. On arrival, he settled in the village of Nazareth. This move was a fulfillment of the prophetic words, "He shall be called a Nazarene."

(Matthew 2:1–23)

There the child grew
strong in body and wise in spirit.
And the grace of God was on him.

LUKE 2:40

A green Shoot will sprout

from Jesse's stump,

from his roots a budding Branch.

The life-giving Spirit of GOD

will hover over him,

the Spirit that brings wisdom

and understanding,

The Spirit that gives direction

and builds strength,

the Spirit that instills knowledge

and Fear-of-GOD.

Isaiah 11:1

Who we are
and will be is compounded with
who God is and what he does....
God is the center
from which all life develops.

—EUGENE H. PETERSON

Advent Readings

God loves us as children whose destinies
he carries in his heart.

ADVENT READINGS

Reading 1

But when the time arrived that was set by God the Father, God sent his Son, born among us of a woman, born under the conditions of the law so that he might redeem those of us who have been kidnapped by the law. Thus we have been set free to experience our rightful heritage. You can tell for sure that you are now fully adopted as his own children because God sent the Spirit of his Son into our lives crying out, "Papa! Father!" Doesn't that privilege of intimate conversation with God make it plain that you are not a slave, but a child? And if you are a child, you're also an heir, with complete access to the inheritance.

GALATIANS 4:4–7

In his Son, Jesus, he personally took on the human condition, entered the disordered mess of struggling humanity in order to set it right once and for all. The law code, weakened as it always was by fractured human nature, could never have done that.

The law always ended up being used as a Band-Aid on sin instead of a deep healing of it.

ROMANS 8:3–4

Reading 2

You don't need a telescope, a microscope, or a horoscope to realize the fullness of Christ, and the emptiness of the universe without him. When you come to him, that fullness comes together for you, too. His power extends over everything.

COLOSSIANS 2:8–9

The sacred writings contain preliminary reports by the prophets on God's Son. His descent from David roots him in history; his unique identity as Son of God was shown by the Spirit when Jesus was raised from the dead, setting him apart as the Messiah, our Master. Through him we received both the generous gift of his life and the urgent task of passing it on to others who receive it by entering into obedient trust in Jesus. You are who you are through this gift and call of Jesus Christ! And I greet you now with all the generosity of God our Father and our Master Jesus, the Messiah.

ROMANS 1:3–7

Reading 3

"GOD, King of Israel,
your Redeemer, GOD-of-the-Angel-Armies, says:
"I'm first, I'm last, and everything in between.
I'm the only God there is.
Who compares with me?
Speak up. See if you measure up.
From the beginning, who else has always announced what's coming?

So what is coming next? Anybody want to venture a try?
Don't be afraid, and don't worry:
Haven't I always kept you informed, told you what was going on?
You're my eyewitnesses:
Have you ever come across a God, a real God, other than me?
There's no Rock like me that I know of."

ISAIAH 44:6–8

Reading 4

Since the One who saves and those who are saved have a common origin, Jesus doesn't hesitate to treat them as family, saying,

I'll tell my good friends, my brothers and sisters, all I know about you;
I'll join them in worship and praise to you. . . .

Since the children are made of flesh and blood, it's logical that the Savior took on flesh and blood in order to rescue them by his death. By embracing death, taking it into himself, he destroyed the Devil's hold on death and freed all who cower through life, scared to death of death.

It's obvious, of course, that he didn't go to all this trouble for angels. It was for people like us, children of Abraham. That's why he had to enter into every detail of human life. Then, when he came before God as high priest to get rid of the people's sins, he would have already experienced it all himself—all the pain, all the testing—and would be able to help where help was needed.

HEBREWS 2:11–18

Reading 5

If God didn't hesitate to put everything on the line for us, embracing our condition and exposing himself to the worst by sending his own Son, is there anything else he wouldn't gladly and freely do for us?

ROMANS 8:32

This Christian life is a great mystery, far exceeding our understanding, but some things are clear enough:

He appeared in a human body,
was proved right by the invisible Spirit,
was seen by angels.
He was proclaimed among all kinds of peoples,
believed in all over the world,
taken up into heavenly glory.

1 TIMOTHY 3:16

Reading 6

We look at this Son and see the God who cannot be seen. We look at this Son and see God's original purpose in everything created. For everything, absolutely everything, above and below, visible and invisible, rank after rank after rank of angels—*everything* got started in him and finds its purpose in him. He was there before any of it came into existence and holds it all together right up to this moment. And when it comes to the church, he organizes and holds it together, like a head does a body.

He was supreme in the beginning and—leading the resurrection parade—he is supreme in the end. From beginning to end he's there, towering far above everything, everyone. So spacious is he, so roomy, that everything of God finds its proper place in him without crowding. Not only that, but all the broken and dislocated pieces of the universe—people and things, animals and atoms—get properly fixed and fit together in vibrant harmonies, all because of his death, his blood that poured down from the Cross.

COLOSSIANS 1:15–19

Reading 7

No one's ever seen or heard anything like this,
Never so much as imagined anything quite like it—
What God has arranged for those who love him.

1 CORINTHIANS 2:9

He wants not only us but *everyone* saved, you know, everyone to get to know the truth *we've* learned: that there's one God and only one, and one Priest-Mediator between God and us—Jesus, who offered himself in exchange for everyone held captive by sin, to set them all free. Eventually the news is going to get out. This and this only has been my appointed work: getting this news to those who have never heard of God, and explaining how it works by simple faith and plain truth.

1 TIMOTHY 2:5–7

Reading 8

We weren't, you know, just wishing on a star when we laid the facts out before you regarding the powerful return of our Master, Jesus Christ. We were there for the preview! We saw it with our own eyes: Jesus resplendent with light from God the Father as the voice of Majestic Glory spoke: "This is my Son, marked by my love, focus of all my delight." We were there on the holy mountain with him. We heard the voice out of heaven with our very own ears.

We couldn't be more sure of what we saw and heard—*God's* glory, *God's* voice. The prophetic Word was confirmed to us. You'll do well to keep focusing on it. It's the one light you have in a dark time as you wait for daybreak and the rising of the Morning Star in your hearts.

2 PETER 1:16–19

Reading 9

"This is my Son, marked by my love. Listen to him."

MARK 9:7

The Word was first,
the Word present to God,
God present to the Word.
The Word was God,
in readiness for God from day one.

Everything was created through him;
nothing—not one thing!—
came into being without him.
What came into existence was Life,
and the Life was Light to live by.

JOHN 1:1–4

Reading 10

We don't have a priest who is out of touch with our reality. He's been through weakness and testing, experienced it all—all but the sin. So let's walk right up to him and get what he is so ready to give. Take the mercy, accept the help.

HEBREWS 4:15–16

No one has ever gone up into the presence of God except the One who came down from that Presence, the Son of Man. In the same way that Moses lifted the serpent in the desert so people could have something to see and then believe, it is necessary for the Son of Man to be lifted up—and everyone who looks up to him, trusting and expectant, will gain a real life, eternal life.

This is how much God loved the world: He gave his Son, his one and only Son. And this is why: so that no one need be destroyed; by believing in him, anyone can have a whole and lasting life. God didn't go to all the trouble of sending his Son merely to point an accusing finger, telling the world how bad it was. He came to help, to put the world right again.

JOHN 3:13–17

Reading 11

The Word became flesh and blood,
and moved into the neighborhood.
We saw the glory with our own eyes,
the one-of-a-kind glory,
like Father, like Son,
Generous inside and out,
true from start to finish.

JOHN 1:14

By his Son, God created the world in the beginning, and it will all belong to the Son at the end. This Son perfectly mirrors God, and is stamped with God's nature. He holds everything together by what he says—powerful words!

HEBREWS 1:2–3

Reading 12

Father, it's time.
Display the bright splendor of your Son
So the Son in turn may show your bright splendor.
You put him in charge of everything human
So he might give real and eternal life to all in his charge.
And this is the real and eternal life:

That they know you,
The one and only true God,
And Jesus Christ, whom you sent.
I glorified you on earth
By completing down to the last detail
What you assigned me to do.
And now, Father, glorify me with your very own splendor,
The very splendor I had in your presence
Before there was a world.
I spelled out your character in detail
To the men and women you gave me.
They were yours in the first place;
Then you gave them to me,
And they have now done what you said.
They know now, beyond the shadow of a doubt,
That everything you gave me is firsthand from you,
For the message you gave me, I gave them;
And they took it, and were convinced
That I came from you.
They believed that you sent me.

JOHN 17:1–8

Reading 13

"I left the Father and arrived in the world. . . ."

JOHN 16:28

"I came down from heaven not to follow my own whim but to accomplish the will of the One who sent me."

JOHN 6:38

So he became their Savior.
In all their troubles,
he was troubled, too.
He didn't send someone else to help them.
He did it himself, in person.
Out of his own love and pity
he redeemed them.

ISAIAH 63:8–9

Reading 14

Christ came and preached peace to you outsiders and peace to us insiders. He treated us as equals, and so made us equals. Through him we both share the same Spirit and have equal access to the Father.

EPHESIANS 2:17–18

Since Jesus went through everything you're going through and more, learn to think like him. Think of your sufferings as a weaning from that old sinful habit of always expecting to get your own way. Then you'll be able to live out your days free to pursue what God wants instead of being tyrannized by what you want.

1 PETER 4:1–2

Reading 15

Fear not, earth! Be glad and celebrate!
GOD has done great things.
Fear not, wild animals!
The fields and meadows are greening up.
The trees are bearing fruit again:
a bumper crop of fig trees and vines!
Children of Zion, celebrate!
Be glad in your GOD.
He's giving you a teacher
to train you how to live right—
Teaching, like rain out of heaven, showers of words
to refresh and nourish your soul, just as he used to do.

JOEL 2:21–23

Reading 16

"You are my Son, chosen and marked by my love, pride of my life."

MARK 1:11

"I promise in my own name:
Every word out of my mouth does what it says.
I never take back what I say.
Everyone is going to end up kneeling before me.
Everyone is going to end up saying of me,
'Yes! Salvation and strength are in GOD!'"

ISAIAH 45:23–24

Reading 17

We've seen for ourselves and continue to state openly that the Father sent his Son as Savior of the world. Everyone who confesses that Jesus is God's Son participates continuously in an intimate relationship with God. We know it so well, we've embraced it heart and soul, this love that comes from God.

1 JOHN 4:14-16

But to us who are personally called by God himself—both Jews and Greeks—Christ is God's ultimate miracle and wisdom all wrapped up in one. Human wisdom is so tinny, so impotent, next to the seeming absurdity of God. Human strength can't begin to compete with God's "weakness."

1 CORINTHIANS 1:24

Reading 18

"The Bread of God came down out of heaven and is giving life to the world."

JOHN 6:33

Your throne is God's throne,
ever and always;
The scepter of your royal rule
measures right living.
You love the right
and hate the wrong.
And that is why God, your very own God,
poured fragrant oil on your head,
Marking you out as king
from among your dear companions.

PSALM 45:6–7

Reading 19

You are familiar with the generosity of our Master, Jesus Christ. Rich as he was, he gave it all away for us—in one stroke he became poor and we became rich.

2 CORINTHIANS 8:9

It's true, is it not, that the One who climbed up also climbed down, down to the valley of earth? And the One who climbed down is the One who climbed back up, up to highest heaven. He handed out gifts above and below, filled heaven with his gifts, filled earth with his gifts.

EPHESIANS 4:9-10

Reading 20

Jesus resumed talking to the people, but now tenderly. "The Father has given me all these things to do and say. This is a unique Father-Son operation, coming out of Father and Son intimacies and knowledge. No one knows the Son the way the Father does, nor the Father the way the Son does. But I'm not keeping it to myself; I'm ready to go over it line by line with anyone willing to listen.

"Are you tired? Worn out? Burned out on religion? Come to me. Get away with me and you'll recover your life. I'll show you how to take a real rest. Walk with me and work with me—watch how I do it. Learn the unforced rhythms of grace. I won't lay anything heavy or ill-fitting on you. Keep company with me and you'll learn to live freely and lightly."

MATTHEW 11:27-30

Reading 21

Did God ever say to an angel, "You're my Son; today I celebrate you"? Or, "I'm his Father, he's my Son"? When he presents his honored Son to the world, he says, "All angels must worship him."

HEBREWS 1:5-6

From the very first day, we were there, taking it all in—we heard it with our own ears, saw it with our own eyes, verified it with our own hands. The Word of Life appeared right before our eyes; we saw it happen! And now we're telling you in most sober prose that what we witnessed was, incredibly, this: The infinite Life of God himself took shape before us.

We saw it, we heard it, and now we're telling you so you can experience it along with us, this experience of communion with the Father and his Son, Jesus Christ. Our motive for writing is simply this: We want you to enjoy this, too. Your joy will double our joy!

1 JOHN 1:1–4

Reading 22

When he finally arrives, blazing in beauty and all his angels with him, the Son of Man will take his place on his glorious throne. Then all the nations will be arranged before him and he will sort the people out, much as a shepherd sorts out sheep and goats, putting sheep to his right and goats to his left.

"Then the King will say to those on his right, 'Enter, you who are blessed by my Father! Take what's coming to you in this kingdom. It's been ready for you since the world's foundation. And here's why:

I was hungry and you fed me,
I was thirsty and you gave me a drink,
I was homeless and you gave me a room,
I was shivering and you gave me clothes,
I was sick and you stopped to visit,
I was in prison and you came to me."

MATTHEW 25:31–36

Reading 23

Every high priest selected to represent men and women before God and offer sacrifices for their sins should be able to deal gently with their failings, since he knows what it's like from his own experience. But that also means that he has to offer sacrifices for his own sins as well as the people's.

No one elects himself to this honored position. He's called to it by God, as Aaron was. Neither did Christ presume to set himself up as high priest, but was set apart by the One who said to him, "You're my Son; today I celebrate you!" In another place God declares, "You're a priest forever in the royal order of Melchizedek."

While he lived on earth, anticipating death, Jesus cried out in pain and wept in sorrow as he offered up priestly prayers to God. Because he honored God, God answered him. Though he was God's Son, he learned trusting-obedience by what he suffered, just as we do. Then, having arrived at the full stature of his maturity and having been announced by God as high priest in the order of Melchizedek, he became the source of eternal salvation to all who believingly obey him.

HEBREWS 5:1–10

Reading 24

Think of yourselves the way Christ Jesus thought of himself. He had equal status with God but didn't think so much of himself that he had to cling to the advantages of that status no matter what. Not at all. When the time came, he set aside the privileges of deity and took on the status of a slave, became *human!* Having become human, he stayed human. It was an incredibly humbling process. He didn't claim special privileges. Instead, he lived a selfless, obedient life and then died a selfless, obedient death—and the worst kind of death at that: a crucifixion.

Because of that obedience, God lifted him high and honored him far beyond anyone or anything, ever, so that all created beings in heaven and on earth—even those long ago dead and buried—will bow in worship before this Jesus Christ, and call out in praise that he is the Master of all, to the glorious honor of God the Father.

PHILIPPIANS 2:5–11

Reading 25

My beloved friends, let us continue to love each other since love comes from God. Everyone who loves is born of God and experiences a relationship with God. The person who refuses to love doesn't know the first thing about God, because God is love—so you can't know him if you don't love. This is how God showed his love for us: God sent his only Son into the world so we might live through him. This is the kind of love we are talking about—not that we once upon a time loved God, but that he loved us and sent his Son as a sacrifice to clear away our sins and the damage they've done to our relationship with God.

My dear, dear friends, if God loved us like this, we certainly ought to love each other. No one has seen God, ever. But if we love one another, God dwells deeply within us, and his love becomes complete in us—perfect love!

1 JOHN 4:7–12

Reading 26

So Jesus explained himself at length. "I'm telling you this straight. The Son can't independently do a thing, only what he sees the Father doing. What the Father does, the Son does. The Father loves the Son and includes him in everything he is doing.

"But you haven't seen the half of it yet, for in the same way that the Father raises the dead and creates life, so does the Son. The Son gives life to anyone he chooses. Neither he nor the Father shuts anyone out. The Father handed all authority to judge over to the Son so that the Son will be honored equally with the Father. Anyone who dishonors the Son, dishonors the Father, for it was the Father's decision to put the Son in the place of honor."

JOHN 5:19–23

Reading 27

Jesus said, "I am the Road, also the Truth, also the Life. No one gets to the Father apart from me. If you really knew me, you would know my Father as well. From now on, you do know him. You've even seen him!"

Philip said, "Master, show us the Father; then we'll be content."

"You've been with me all this time, Philip, and you still don't understand? To see me is to see the Father. So how can you ask, 'Where is the Father?' Don't you believe that I am in the Father and the Father is in me? The words that I speak to you aren't mere words. I don't just make them up on my own. The Father who resides in me crafts each word into a divine act.

"Believe me: I am in my Father and my Father is in me."

JOHN 14:7–11

Reading 28

Wake up, you sleepyhead city!
Wake up, you sleepyhead people!
King-Glory is ready to enter.
Who is this King-Glory?
GOD, armed
and battle-ready.
Wake up, you sleepyhead city!
Wake up, you sleepyhead people!
King-Glory is ready to enter.
Who is this King-Glory?
GOD of the angel armies:
he is King-Glory.

PSALM 24:7–10